# THE
# **SKILLET SUPPER**
## COOKBOOK

DEVELOPED BY
WILLIAMS
SONOMA
TEST KITCHEN

**PHOTOGRAPHS** Aubrie Pick

weldon**owen**

# CONTENTS

# THE MIGHTY SKILLET

Essential to any well-stocked kitchen, skillets are endlessly versatile pieces of cookware that you'll turn to again and again. Reliable, durable, and easy to clean, these multitaskers yield superb results whether you're frying, sautéing, roasting, braising, or baking. In the Williams-Sonoma Test Kitchen, where we develop hundreds of recipes every year, we reach for our skillets frequently to prepare a wide variety of dishes— from steak and salmon to eggs, pizza, and grilled cheese sandwiches. Skillets are also perfect for one-dish meals.

On the following pages, you'll find more than 20 delicious skillet-cooked recipes that are ideal for many occasions. Pair the Frittata with Chard, Sausage & Feta (page 45) with a salad for an easy Sunday supper. For movie night, go with an updated classic—Grilled Cheese with Bacon, Avocado & Spinach (page 20)—or serve up tasty Chicken & Cheese Enchiladas (page 28). Weeknights, try Soy-Ginger Glazed Salmon with Broccolini (page 33), Korean Chicken Fajitas (page 48), or Maple-Rosemary Pork Tenderloin with Smashed Potatoes (page 31). For entertaining guests, Steak au Poivre with Red Wine & Mushroom Pan Sauce (page 24) is perfect. And for a fun family-night supper, make Pesto Pizza with Zucchini & Cherry Tomatoes (page 34). Whatever recipe you choose, your skillet will be your go-to pan for excellent meals.

# SKILLET PRIMER

A skillet is a broad pan with a flat bottom and sides that flare out, making it easy to turn and toss food and to slide it out of the pan. Skillets come in a range of sizes (typically from 7 to 12 inches) and materials, including stainless-steel, cast iron, nonstick, and copper. It's useful to have several skillets on hand—one small, one medium, and one large. If you buy only two skillets, make one of them nonstick. Skillets can come with lids, which are handy for covered cooking. Properly cared for, a high-quality skillet will last a lifetime and provide consistently outstanding results.

## STAINLESS-STEEL SKILLETS

Stainless steel is extremely durable and attractive. Easy to clean, stainless-steel skillets are an invaluable and long-lasting addition to any kitchen. When bonded with aluminum or copper, stainless steel distributes heat evenly and works on any stove top, including induction. Most stainless-steel skillets are also safe to use in a broiler. While stainless-steel pans are dishwasher safe, most manufacturers recommend washing them by hand using warm, soapy water.

## CAST-IRON SKILLETS Generations

of cooks have used cast-iron skillets to prepare everything from bacon to biscuits, and well-seasoned heirloom pans are often handed down in families. You can cook almost anything in a cast-iron skillet, although some manufacturers recommend that you avoid cooking acidic ingredients in a new cast-iron pan because they will react with the material, affecting the flavor and color of the food. (Once the pan is well seasoned, it's fine to cook acidic foods in it.) Cast-iron skillets heat evenly and work on any stove top, including induction, and can go from oven to table for convenient serving. Wash cast-iron skillets by hand.

Enameled cast-iron skillets are a stylish alternative to traditional cast-iron skillets. They're available in a range of vibrant colors including red, green, orange, and blue and, like traditional cast-iron skillets, can go from oven to table, making them an attractive tabletop showpiece. Enameled cast-iron skillets do not require seasoning and will not react with acidic food. They are dishwasher safe, but washing them by hand is usually recommended.

## NONSTICK SKILLETS  A skillet with

a nonstick coating releases foods easily and cleanly, making the pan easier to wash after cooking. When you're cooking with a nonstick skillet, be sure to use a rubber spatula or a wooden spoon so you don't scratch the surface. Nonstick skillets are excellent for gas and electric stove tops, but not all nonstick skillets are suitable for induction stove tops, so be sure to check the manufacturer's product information for your skillet before using it on an induction range. Like cast-iron skillets, nonstick skillets should be washed by hand.

## COPPER SKILLETS  Copper is an

excellent conductor of heat, and copper skillets work on any stove top, including induction. Copper's lustrous appearance makes it a favorite in many kitchens, but it requires more care and maintenance than stainless steel—it scratches easily and needs regular polishing to maintain its luster. Wash copper skillets by hand.

Stainless steel

Cast-iron

Nonstick

Copper

# CARING FOR YOUR SKILLETS

- To prevent skillets from warping, never place a hot pan under cold water. Allow the pan to cool completely before cleaning. To prevent spotting, rinse the pan in hot water and dry immediately.

- Hand wash a new cast-iron skillet before its first use and dry immediately. Rub the pan with a light coat of vegetable oil after every wash. (Enameled cast-iron skillets do not need to be seasoned.)

- If you're using a cast-iron skillet as a serving dish, be sure to protect your tabletop by setting the hot skillet on a trivet.

- Avoid using a new cast-iron skillet to cook acidic foods, such as tomatoes and some sauces; they can damage the pan's seasoning. Once the seasoning is well established, it's fine to cook acidic foods in the skillet.

- To maintain a copper skillet's lustrous appearance, polish it regularly using a good-quality copper cleaner.

For extra flavor, place peeled garlic cloves, fresh thyme sprigs, and a lemon half in the chicken cavity before roasting.

# ROASTED CHICKEN WITH FINGERLING POTATOES & CARROTS

For a more colorful dish, use a mix of purple, dark red, orange, and bright yellow carrots. You can add a handful of unpeeled garlic cloves with the other vegetables and invite guests to squeeze the caramelized cloves from their papery skins and spread them on crusty bread.

**1** Preheat the oven to 450°F.

**2** In a small bowl, stir together the butter, ½ teaspoon pepper, the paprika, cumin, and coriander until well blended. Pat the chicken dry and rub the seasoned butter evenly on the outside of the chicken. Season generously with salt.

**3** In a large bowl, toss together the potatoes, carrots, shallots, and oil, and season generously with salt and pepper. Transfer the vegetables to a large ovenproof skillet and spread in a single layer. Place the chicken on top of the vegetables.

**4** Reduce the oven temperature to 400°F and transfer the skillet to the oven. Roast until an instant-read thermometer inserted into the thickest part of the thigh, away from the bone, registers 165°F, 50–65 minutes.

**5** Transfer the chicken to a cutting board, cover loosely with aluminum foil, and let rest for 10–15 minutes before carving. Insert a small, sharp knife into the potatoes; it should slide through easily. If not, return the skillet to the oven and roast the potatoes for 10–15 minutes longer.

**6** Carve the chicken and serve the vegetables alongside.

|||||||||||||||||||||||||||||||||||||||||||||||||||||||||||||||||||||||||

4 tablespoons unsalted butter, at room temperature

Kosher salt and freshly ground pepper

½ teaspoon smoked paprika

¼ teaspoon ground cumin

¼ teaspoon ground coriander

1 whole chicken (3–4 lb)

1 lb fingerling potatoes, cut into 2-inch pieces

1 bunch carrots, peeled and left whole or cut into 2-inch pieces

2 large shallots, cut into ¼-inch slices

2 tablespoons olive oil

**SERVES 4**

# HALIBUT WITH LEMON, HERBS & SAUTÉED ASPARAGUS

The versatile skillet does triple duty here: it is used first for sautéing the asparagus, then for steaming the fish, and finally for simmering the sauce. Serve this elegant dish with steamed fingerling potatoes tossed with butter and parsley, and pour a light, crisp white wine.

|||||||||||||||||||||||||||||||||||||||||||||||||||||||||||||

3 tablespoons olive oil

½ lb asparagus, trimmed and thinly sliced on the diagonal

Kosher salt and freshly ground pepper

4 halibut fillets (about 6 oz each)

1 cup white wine

4 tablespoons fresh lemon juice

2 shallots, minced

1 lemon, sliced

4 tablespoons unsalted butter, cut into pieces

2 tablespoons minced fresh dill

1 tablespoon minced fresh flat-leaf parsley

2 tablespoons pine nuts, toasted

Thinly shaved fennel, for garnish (optional)

**SERVES 4**

**1** In a large nonstick skillet over medium-high heat, warm 1 tablespoon of the oil. Add the asparagus and a pinch each of salt and pepper. Cook, stirring occasionally, until the asparagus is lightly browned and just tender, 6–8 minutes. Transfer to a serving platter and cover with aluminum foil.

**2** Season the halibut with salt and pepper. In the same skillet over medium heat, warm 1 tablespoon of the oil. Place the halibut in the skillet and add ½ cup of the wine and 2 tablespoons of the lemon juice. Cover and steam until the fish is cooked through, 8–10 minutes, adding ½ cup water if the liquid evaporates before the fish is done. Transfer the fish to the platter with the asparagus and cover with aluminum foil.

**3** In the same skillet over medium heat, warm the remaining 1 tablespoon oil. Add the shallots, lemon slices, and a pinch of salt and cook, stirring occasionally, until slightly translucent, 3–4 minutes. Add the remaining ½ cup wine and 2 tablespoons lemon juice and cook until reduced by half, 3–4 minutes. Remove from the heat, add the butter, and stir until melted. Stir in the dill and parsley, and season with salt and pepper. Pour the sauce over the fish and asparagus. Garnish with the pine nuts and fennel, if using.

To test the fish for doneness, insert a small, sharp knife into the thickest part; if there is any resistance, continue cooking the fish.

For a delicious variation, replace the beef with thinly sliced boneless chicken or peeled and deveined shrimp.

# STIR-FRIED BEEF WITH BELL PEPPERS & BASIL

A well-seasoned cast-iron skillet is a great stand-in for a wok. Before you begin prepping the ingredients for this dish, put a pot of rice on to cook, and it should be ready when the stir-fry is done.

**1** In a small bowl, stir together the soy sauce, fish sauce, oyster sauce, and sugar. Set aside.

**2** In a large cast-iron skillet over medium-high heat, warm the oil. Add the steak and cook, stirring frequently, until cooked through, 1–2 minutes. Transfer the steak to a platter. Add the bell pepper and onion to the skillet and cook, stirring occasionally, until the vegetables are slightly softened, about 5 minutes. Add the garlic and ginger and stir-fry for 1 minute.

**3** Return the steak to the skillet. Add the lime juice and half of the soy sauce mixture and toss until warmed through. Garnish with basil and serve with the remaining sauce and lime wedges alongside.

7 tablespoons soy sauce

2 tablespoons Asian fish sauce

2 teaspoons oyster sauce

2 teaspoons sugar

2 tablespoons vegetable oil

1 lb flank steak, thinly sliced across the grain

1 red bell pepper, seeded and thinly sliced

1 yellow onion, thinly sliced

4 cloves garlic, minced

1 tablespoon peeled and grated fresh ginger

Juice of ½ lime

Fresh basil leaves, for garnish

Lime wedges, for serving

**SERVES 4**

# BAKED EGGS IN TOMATO SAUCE

This recipe is an adaptation of shakshouka, a homey classic of North Africa. The dish tastes best when the egg whites are set but the yolks are still fluid. Bread is indispensable for sopping up the flavorful sauce and the rich, runny yolks.

|||||||||||||||||||||||||||||||||||||||||||||||||||||||||||||

2 tablespoons olive oil

1 yellow onion, diced

1 red bell pepper, seeded and thinly sliced

3 cloves garlic, minced

1 jalapeño chile, seeded and diced

1 tablespoon sweet paprika

1 tablespoon ground cumin

1 teaspoon fennel seeds

1 teaspoon anchovy paste

2 tablespoons tomato paste

1 can (28 oz) whole peeled tomatoes

3 tablespoons sugar

Kosher salt and freshly ground pepper

6 large eggs

½ cup crumbled feta cheese

2 tablespoons fresh cilantro leaves, for garnish

Crusty bread, for serving

**SERVES 4–6**

**1** Preheat the oven to 375°F.

**2** In a medium ovenproof nonstick skillet over medium-high heat, warm the oil. Add the onion and bell pepper and cook, stirring occasionally, until the onion is translucent and the pepper is tender, 4–6 minutes. Add the garlic, jalapeño, paprika, cumin, and fennel seeds and cook, stirring occasionally, for 2 minutes. Add the anchovy paste, tomato paste, tomatoes and their juices, sugar, and a large pinch each of salt and pepper. Cook for 2 minutes, breaking the tomatoes apart with the back of a spoon. Use the back of a spoon to create 6 wells in the tomatoes, carefully crack the eggs, and place one in each well.

**3** Transfer to the oven and bake until the eggs are set, about 10 minutes. Sprinkle with the cheese, cilantro, and a large pinch each of salt and pepper. Serve warm with crusty bread.

This dish is wonderful for brunch. Prepare the tomato sauce the night before and refrigerate, then add the eggs the next day and bake.

# GRILLED CHEESE WITH BACON, AVOCADO & SPINACH

Here, the old-fashioned grilled cheese, a favorite of soup-and-sandwich suppers, gets a creative makeover with lots of tasty add-ins. If you have vegetarians at your table, skip the bacon. The sandwiches will still be sublime. Substitute smoked Gouda for the mozzarella if you like.

½ lb goat cheese, at room temperature

1½ tablespoons heavy cream, plus more as needed

2 tablespoons chopped fresh basil

1 tablespoon chopped fresh dill

1 tablespoon chopped fresh flat-leaf parsley

Kosher salt and freshly ground pepper

8 slices bacon

8 slices seeded bread

1 avocado, pitted, peeled, and thinly sliced

¾ lb mozzarella or Monterey jack cheese, thinly sliced

2 cups baby spinach

2 tablespoons olive oil

**SERVES 4**

**1** Preheat the oven to 200°F.

**2** In a bowl, stir together the goat cheese and cream until smooth and spreadable, adding more cream if needed. Stir in the basil, dill, and parsley, and season with salt and pepper. Set aside.

**3** In a large skillet over medium heat, cook the bacon, turning once, until crispy, about 8 minutes. Transfer to a paper towel–lined plate. Pour off the fat from the skillet and wipe out the skillet with a paper towel.

**4** Spread the herbed goat cheese on one side of the bread slices. Arrange the avocado on 4 of the slices and season with salt and pepper. For each sandwich, top the avocado with 2 bacon slices (cut in half if needed to fit) and then with the mozzarella and spinach, dividing evenly. Cover each with one of the remaining bread slices, goat cheese–side down, and press together gently.

**5** In the same skillet over medium-low heat, warm 1 tablespoon of the oil. Add 2 of the sandwiches and cook until golden brown and crisp underneath, 3–4 minutes. Flip the sandwiches and cook until the second side is golden brown and the cheese is melted, 3–4 minutes longer. Transfer to a plate and keep warm in the oven. Using the remaining 1 tablespoon oil, repeat to cook the remaining 2 sandwiches. If the cheese has not completely melted, leave the sandwiches in the oven for 5 minutes longer.

# SPICY PORK LETTUCE CUPS

When serving this Asian-inspired recipe, invite guests to spoon the pork mixture into a lettuce "cup," drizzle it with the soy mixture, overlap the top of the leaf, and eat the packet out of hand. And yes, drips are inevitable, so offer plenty of napkins.

**1** In a large skillet over medium-high heat, warm the vegetable oil. Add the green onions, ginger, garlic, lemongrass, red pepper flakes, and mushrooms and cook, stirring occasionally, until the mushrooms are soft, 2–3 minutes. Add the ground pork and cook, stirring occasionally, until golden brown and cooked through, 8–10 minutes. Stir in the water chestnuts.

**2** In a small bowl, whisk together the soy sauce, vinegar, sesame oil, fish sauce, and brown sugar.

**3** Add half of the soy sauce mixture to the pork mixture and toss to combine. Garnish with cilantro. Serve with the lettuce leaves and the remaining soy sauce mixture, and let diners assemble their own lettuce cups.

2 tablespoons vegetable oil

½ cup sliced green onions, white parts only

1½ tablespoons peeled and grated fresh ginger

2 cloves garlic, minced

2 tablespoons minced lemongrass

Pinch of red pepper flakes

¼ lb shiitake mushrooms, stemmed and minced

1 lb ground pork

½ cup water chestnuts, roughly chopped

6 tablespoons soy sauce

2 tablespoons rice vinegar

2 tablespoons toasted sesame oil

1 tablespoon Asian fish sauce

2 teaspoons firmly packed light brown sugar

Fresh cilantro leaves, for garnish

1–2 heads butter lettuce, leaves separated

**SERVES 4**

# SKILLET SAUSAGE & BEEF LASAGNE

A big lasagne supper too often means a full kitchen sink. But here, the same ovenproof skillet is used for making the sauce and baking the lasagne. Be sure to cover the top pasta layer completely with sauce so it will cook evenly.

**1** Preheat the oven to 375°F.

**2** In a large cast-iron skillet over medium-high heat, warm the oil. Add the sausage and ground beef and cook, stirring occasionally, until browned, 4–6 minutes. Transfer to a plate. Pour off all but 1 tablespoon of the fat from the skillet.

**3** Return the skillet to medium-high heat, add the onion and garlic, and cook, stirring occasionally, until the onion is translucent, 4–6 minutes. Add the oregano and red pepper flakes and cook, stirring occasionally, for 30 seconds. Add the tomatoes and the sausage mixture, and season with salt and black pepper. Transfer the sauce to a large bowl.

**4** In a medium bowl, stir together the basil, ricotta, 1 cup of the mozzarella, ¼ cup of the Parmesan, the egg, and a large pinch each of salt and black pepper.

**5** Spread ⅓ cup of the sauce evenly on the bottom of the skillet. Cover with a single layer of 3 lasagne noodles (break up noodles into smaller pieces to fill in any gaps). Top with ⅓ cup of the ricotta mixture, ⅓ cup of the sauce, ¾ cup of the mozzarella, ¼ cup of the Parmesan, and another layer of 3 lasagne noodles. Repeat the layering of sauce, noodles, ricotta mixture, and cheeses 3 more times. Cover with the remaining 3 lasagne noodles, then top with the remaining sauce, mozzarella, and Parmesan.

**6** Transfer to the oven and bake until the lasagne is browned and bubbly, about 45 minutes. Let rest for 15 minutes before slicing. Garnish with basil and serve.

2 tablespoons olive oil

½ lb pork sausage, casing removed

½ lb ground beef

1 yellow onion, diced

3 cloves garlic, minced

2 teaspoons dried oregano

Pinch of red pepper flakes

1 can (28 oz) crushed tomatoes

Kosher salt and freshly ground black pepper

1 cup packed fresh basil leaves, roughly chopped, plus whole basil leaves for garnish

1 package (15 oz) ricotta cheese

4 ½ cups shredded mozzarella cheese

1 ½ cups grated Parmesan cheese

1 large egg, lightly beaten

15 no-boil lasagne noodles

**SERVES 6–8**

# STEAK AU POIVRE WITH RED WINE & MUSHROOM PAN SAUCE

In place of the beef tenderloin called for here, feel free to use New York strip steaks. They come from the same part of the steer, the short loin, but have more marbling, a bit more bite, and a more robust flavor.

**FOR THE HERB BUTTER**

2 tablespoons unsalted butter, at room temperature

½ teaspoon minced fresh rosemary

½ teaspoon minced fresh flat-leaf parsley

1 clove garlic, minced

Kosher salt and freshly ground pepper

2 tablespoons olive oil

½ lb assorted mushrooms, such as cremini, king oyster, or maitake, thinly sliced

4 tablespoons unsalted butter

4 beef tenderloin steaks (6–8 oz each)

2 shallots, minced

1 cup chicken broth

¼ cup red wine

¼ cup crème fraîche or heavy cream

Kosher salt and freshly ground pepper

**SERVES 4**

**1** To make the herb butter, in a small bowl, stir together the butter, rosemary, parsley, and garlic, and season with salt and pepper. Form into a log, wrap in plastic wrap, and refrigerate until ready to serve.

**2** Preheat the oven to 400°F. In a large ovenproof skillet over medium heat, warm 1 tablespoon of the oil. Add the mushrooms and cook, stirring, until golden brown and tender, 6–8 minutes. Transfer to a plate.

**3** Season the steaks with salt and pepper. In the same skillet used for the mushrooms, over medium-high heat, melt 2 tablespoons of the butter with the remaining 1 tablespoon oil until shimmering. Add the steaks and sear for 2 minutes per side. Transfer to the oven and roast until the steaks are done to your liking, about 5 minutes for medium-rare. Transfer the steaks to a cutting board and cover loosely with aluminum foil.

**4** Pour off the excess fat from the skillet, place over medium heat, and melt the remaining 2 tablespoons butter. Add the shallots and cook, stirring occasionally, until translucent, about 3 minutes. Add the broth and bring to a simmer. Add the wine and simmer until reduced by half, about 5 minutes. Remove from the heat, stir in the crème fraîche, and season with salt and pepper. Stir in the mushrooms, reheating over medium heat until warmed through, if needed.

**5** Unwrap the herb butter and cut into thin slices. Arrange the steaks, sliced thin across the grain or whole, on a serving platter or individual plates. Top with the mushroom sauce and the herb butter and serve.

To boost the flavor, place a rosemary sprig and a garlic clove in the skillet with the steaks. After flipping them, tilt the pan so the butter pools and use a spoon to baste the steaks before transferring to the oven.

For a gluten-free dish, replace the soy sauce with tamari. You can also substitute sautéed chicken or panfried tofu for the shrimp.

# FRIED RICE WITH SHRIMP & BROCCOLINI

Fried rice cooks up effortlessly in a big nonstick skillet. The pan's sloped sides make it easy to turn and toss the rice without it tumbling out, and the nonstick surface ensures the grains take on a little color but don't burn.

**1** Pat the shrimp dry and season generously with salt and pepper. In a large nonstick skillet over medium-high heat, warm 1 tablespoon of the vegetable oil. Add the shrimp and cook, turning once, until cooked through, about 3 minutes. Transfer to a plate.

**2** In the same skillet over high heat, warm 1 tablespoon of the vegetable oil. Add the broccolini and cook, stirring occasionally, until tender-crisp, about 3 minutes. Season with salt and pepper and transfer to a plate.

**3** In the same skillet over high heat, warm 1 tablespoon of the vegetable oil. Add the bell pepper and cook, stirring occasionally, until slightly charred and tender-crisp, about 2 minutes. Transfer to the plate with the broccolini.

**4** In the same skillet over medium-high heat, warm the remaining 1 tablespoon vegetable oil. Add the ginger and garlic and cook, stirring occasionally, until fragrant, about 1 minute. Add the rice and cook, stirring occasionally, until lightly golden brown and crisp, about 3 minutes. Add the peas, soy sauce, vinegar, sesame oil, and Sriracha and stir to combine. Add the shrimp and broccolini mixture and toss to combine. Adjust the seasoning with soy sauce or salt and pepper. Transfer to a serving platter and garnish with the cilantro.

¾ lb medium shrimp, peeled and deveined

Kosher salt and freshly ground pepper

4 tablespoons vegetable oil

3 cups chopped broccolini (about 2 bunches)

1 red bell pepper, seeded and thinly sliced

1 tablespoon peeled and minced fresh ginger

1 tablespoon minced garlic

3 cups cooked short-grain white rice, cooled

½ cup frozen peas, thawed

3 tablespoons soy sauce, plus more as needed

2 tablespoons rice vinegar

1 teaspoon toasted sesame oil

1 teaspoon Sriracha chile sauce

2 tablespoons fresh cilantro leaves

**SERVES 4**

# CHICKEN & CHEESE ENCHILADAS

If you'd like to use corn tortillas instead of flour tortillas, wrap the stack of tortillas in aluminum foil and slip them in the preheated oven until they are pliable, about 5 minutes. Corn tortillas fold more easily when they're heated.

1 tablespoon olive oil, plus more for greasing

Kosher salt and freshly ground pepper

1 lb baby spinach

1 yellow onion, diced

1 clove garlic, minced

2 cups shredded cooked chicken

½ cup sour cream

1 cup shredded mozzarella cheese

½ cup shredded white Cheddar cheese

½ cup shredded yellow Cheddar cheese

2 tablespoons chopped fresh cilantro, plus more for garnish

2 cans (15 oz each) green enchilada sauce

6–8 flour tortillas

2 green onions, white and pale green parts, thinly sliced

**SERVES 6–8**

**1** Preheat the oven to 350°F. Lightly grease a large cast-iron skillet.

**2** Bring a large saucepan of salted water to a boil over high heat. Add the spinach and cook until wilted but still bright green, 2–3 minutes. Rinse under cold running water and drain well, then coarsely chop. Set aside.

**3** In a large nonstick skillet over medium-high heat, warm the oil. Add the onion and garlic, season with salt and pepper, and cook, stirring occasionally, until the onion is translucent, 4–6 minutes. Let cool.

**4** In a large bowl, stir together the onion mixture, spinach, chicken, sour cream, half of the mozzarella and Cheddar, and the cilantro.

**5** To assemble the enchiladas, spread 1 cup of the enchilada sauce in the prepared skillet. Pour 2 cups of the sauce into a pie dish or a shallow bowl. Using tongs, dip a tortilla into the sauce. Place the tortilla on a work surface, add a few tablespoons of the chicken filling down the center, and roll up the tortilla. Place the enchilada, seam side down, in the skillet. Repeat with the remaining tortillas and filling. Drizzle all of the remaining sauce, including any left in the pie dish, evenly over the enchiladas, and sprinkle with the remaining mozzarella and Cheddar.

**6** Transfer to the oven and bake until the cheese is melted and the sauce is bubbling, 30–35 minutes. Garnish with the green onions and cilantro and serve right away.

To make vegetarian enchiladas, swap cooked diced vegetables, such as corn, tomatoes, or zucchini, for the chicken.

# CRISPY CHICKEN THIGHS WITH HONEY-LEMON GLAZE

These crispy thighs are brushed with a sweet-salty-tart glaze just before serving. Accompany them with steamed rice laced with toasted pine nuts or walnuts, plus a simple salad of arugula tossed with shaved ricotta salata and a shallot vinaigrette.

8 skin-on, bone-in chicken thighs

Kosher salt and freshly ground pepper

2 tablespoons olive oil

1 yellow onion, thinly sliced

1 fennel bulb, trimmed and thinly sliced

½ cup white wine

1 cup chicken broth, plus more as needed

1 bay leaf

1 lemon, halved

3 cloves garlic

4 fresh thyme sprigs

1 teaspoon Worcestershire sauce (optional)

**FOR THE HONEY-LEMON GLAZE**

¼ cup honey

2 tablespoons fresh lemon juice

1 tablespoon olive oil

1 tablespoon soy sauce

**SERVES 4**

**1** Preheat the oven to 375°F. Pat the chicken dry and season with salt and pepper.

**2** In a large ovenproof skillet over medium-high heat, warm 1 tablespoon of the oil. Working in batches, add the chicken, skin side down, and cook until deep golden brown, 3–4 minutes per batch. Transfer to a plate. Pour off the fat from the skillet.

**3** In the same skillet over medium heat, warm the remaining 1 tablespoon oil. Add the onion, fennel, and a pinch each of salt and pepper. Cook, stirring occasionally, until the vegetables are tender and slightly caramelized, 8–10 minutes. Add the wine and cook, stirring to scrape up the browned bits, until reduced by half, 2–3 minutes. Add the broth, bay leaf, a generous pinch of salt, the lemon halves, garlic, thyme sprigs, and Worcestershire sauce (if using) and bring to a simmer. Remove from the heat and nestle the chicken thighs, skin side up, in the skillet. Add more broth if needed so that the thighs are completely covered, except for the skin.

**4** Transfer to the oven and roast until the chicken is very tender and cooked through, about 1 hour. Using a slotted spoon, transfer the chicken, onion, and fennel to a serving platter.

**5** To make the honey-lemon glaze, in a small bowl, whisk together all the ingredients. Brush the tops of the chicken with the glaze and serve warm.

# MAPLE-ROSEMARY PORK TENDERLOIN WITH SMASHED POTATOES

Pork tenderloin is a lean, mild-flavored, slender cut that can easily dry out if cooked too long, so keep track of the time. If your tenderloin still has its silver skin (sinewy, white membrane) intact, carefully cut it away with a paring knife before marinating.

**1** To make the marinade, in a large bowl, whisk together the oil, mustard, maple syrup, rosemary, and garlic. Season the pork tenderloin with salt and pepper. Add the tenderloin to the marinade, making sure it is completely covered. Let stand at room temperature for 30 minutes or refrigerate up to overnight.

**2** Preheat the oven to 375°F.

**3** In a large bowl, toss the potatoes with 2 tablespoons of the oil and a generous pinch of salt. Remove the tenderloin from the marinade and place in the center of a large ovenproof skillet. Arrange the potatoes on either side of the pork.

**4** Transfer to the oven and roast until an instant-read thermometer inserted into the center of the pork registers 145°F, 45 minutes to 1 hour. Transfer the pork to a cutting board, cover loosely with aluminum foil, and let rest before slicing.

**5** Transfer the potatoes to a plate and gently smash them with a spatula. In the same skillet over medium-high heat, warm the remaining 2 tablespoons oil. Add the potatoes and fry, flipping once, until crispy on both sides, about 3 minutes. Add the brussels sprouts and cook, stirring, until tender, about 2 minutes. Remove from the heat, stir in the mustard (if using), and season with salt and pepper. Thinly slice the pork and serve the potatoes and brussels sprouts alongside.

**FOR THE MARINADE**

¼ cup olive oil

¼ cup Dijon mustard

3 tablespoons maple syrup

2 teaspoons chopped fresh rosemary

4 cloves garlic, smashed

1 pork tenderloin (2 lb)

Kosher salt and freshly ground pepper

1 lb small Yukon gold potatoes

4 tablespoons olive oil

½ lb brussels sprouts, trimmed and thinly sliced

1 tablespoon whole-grain mustard (optional)

SERVES 4

# SOY-GINGER GLAZED SALMON WITH BROCCOLINI

Not all nonstick skillets can take the intense high heat of a broiler, so be sure yours can before you decide to make this healthful, no-fuss dish. You can also use cast iron and brush the fillets with oil. When selecting the salmon, look for bright-colored, moist fillets from wild-caught or responsibly farmed fish.

**1** Preheat the broiler.

**2** To make the glaze, in a large broilerproof nonstick skillet over medium heat, combine the soy sauce, brown sugar, hoisin sauce, ginger, and lime juice and cook, stirring to dissolve the sugar, until the mixture is reduced by half, 1–2 minutes. Transfer the glaze to a small bowl. Wipe out the skillet with a paper towel.

**3** Place the salmon, skin side down, in the skillet and brush with the glaze. Arrange the broccolini around the salmon. Transfer to the broiler and cook until the salmon is flaky and the broccolini is tender, 6–8 minutes. Garnish with sesame seeds and green onions, if using. Serve right away over steamed rice.

||||||||||||||||||||||||||||||||||||||||||||||||||||||||||||||||||||

**FOR THE GLAZE**

½ cup soy sauce

⅓ cup firmly packed light brown sugar

2 tablespoons hoisin sauce

1½ tablespoons peeled and grated fresh ginger

Juice of 1 lime

4 salmon fillets (about 6 oz each)

1 bunch broccolini (about ¾ lb), trimmed and cut into 2-inch pieces

¼ teaspoon sesame seeds, for garnish (optional)

1–2 green onions, white and pale green parts, thinly sliced on the diagonal, for garnish (optional)

Steamed rice, for serving

**SERVES 4**

# PESTO PIZZA WITH ZUCCHINI & CHERRY TOMATOES

In this savvy skillet recipe for pizza, you start the pie in a cold pan on the stove top, where the pan gets good and hot. Then the pizza is finished in the oven, where the toppings cook and the crust crisps and browns beautifully.

|||||||||||||||||||||||||||||||||||||||||||||||||||||||||

1 lb pizza dough, store-bought or homemade

All-purpose flour, for dusting

2 teaspoons olive oil, plus more for brushing

3 tablespoons pesto

1 small zucchini, thinly sliced

2 cups shredded mozzarella cheese

½ red or yellow onion, cut into ½-inch slices

1 cup cherry tomatoes, halved

Kosher salt and freshly ground pepper

Grated Parmesan cheese, for garnish

**SERVES 4 (MAKES 2 10-INCH PIZZAS)**

**1** Divide the pizza dough in half, place on a well-floured surface, and let stand at room temperature for about 20 minutes. Preheat the oven to 425°F.

**2** Using a well-floured rolling pin, roll out each dough half into a 10- to 12-inch round about ½ inch thick.

**3** Sprinkle a pinch of flour evenly across the bottom of a large ovenproof skillet. Fit a dough round in the skillet and place on the stove top over medium heat. Drizzle 1 teaspoon of the oil over the dough, then spread with 1½ tablespoons of the pesto. Arrange half each of the zucchini, mozzarella, onion, and tomatoes over the pesto, and season with salt and pepper. Cook until the crust begins to set, 2–3 minutes.

**4** Transfer to the oven. Bake until the cheese is melted and the crust is crisp and golden brown, 10–12 minutes. Remove from the oven, transfer the pizza to a cutting board, and keep warm.

**5** Let the skillet cool slightly, then repeat with the remaining dough round and toppings.

**6** Brush the pizza crusts with oil, sprinkle the pizzas with Parmesan, and serve.

Customize this pizza however you'd like. Top with thin slices of prosciutto that will crisp in the oven, replace the pesto with a roasted garlic white sauce, or try a simple Margherita pizza with sliced tomatoes, basil, and fresh mozzarella.

The apple chutney can be refrigerated for up to 1 week; bring to room temperature or rewarm before serving.

# CIDER-BRINED PORK CHOPS WITH APPLE CHUTNEY

This easy-to-assemble dish is pure comfort food. The chops require overnight brining before cooking so plan accordingly. If there are no green beans at the market, halved brussels sprouts or sugar snap peas are a good substitute.

**1** To make the brine, in a saucepan over medium-high heat, combine the apple cider, 3 tablespoons salt, peppercorns, and bay leaf and heat until warm, stirring to dissolve the salt. Transfer to a large bowl and let cool to room temperature. Add the pork chops, submerging them completely. Cover and refrigerate overnight.

**2** To make the apple chutney, in a large skillet over medium heat, warm the oil. Add the shallot and cook, stirring occasionally, until slightly translucent, about 3 minutes. Add the apples, cranberries, brown sugar, vinegar, ginger, ¼ teaspoon salt, nutmeg, and mustard seeds (if using). Cook, stirring occasionally, until the apples are tender-crisp, 8–10 minutes. Add the apple cider and bring to a simmer. Cook until slightly thickened, about 3 minutes. Transfer to a bowl and let cool to room temperature. Wipe out the skillet.

**3** Remove the pork chops from the brine and pat dry. Let stand at room temperature for 20 minutes. In the same skillet used for the chutney, over medium-high heat, warm 1 tablespoon of the oil. Add the chops and cook until golden brown on both sides and an instant-read thermometer inserted into the center of the chops registers 145°F, about 3 minutes per side. Transfer to a serving platter, cover with aluminum foil, and let rest.

**4** In the same skillet over medium-high heat, warm the remaining 1 tablespoon oil. Add the green beans and cook, stirring occasionally, until tender-crisp, about 10 minutes. Season with salt and pepper. Serve the pork chops with the apple chutney and green beans.

**FOR THE BRINE**

4 cups apple cider

Kosher salt

8 peppercorns

1 bay leaf

4 bone-in center-cut pork chops (about 7 oz each and ¾ inch thick)

**FOR THE APPLE CHUTNEY**

1 tablespoon olive oil

1 shallot, minced

3 apples, such as Fuji or Pink Lady, peeled, cored, and cut into 1-inch dice

½ cup dried cranberries

¼ cup firmly packed light brown sugar

6 tablespoons apple cider vinegar

2 teaspoons peeled and minced fresh ginger

Kosher salt and freshly ground pepper

¼ teaspoon ground nutmeg

1 tablespoon yellow mustard seeds (optional)

½ cup apple cider

2 tablespoons olive oil

½ lb green beans, trimmed

**SERVES 4**

# PENNE PASTA WITH SUN-DRIED TOMATOES & BURRATA

Here is an inspired way to cut down on dirty pots and save time, energy, and water. Combine the pasta, water, and most of the sauce ingredients in a skillet and cook until the pasta is al dente and the water is absorbed. Supper couldn't be simpler.

1 lb penne pasta

½ yellow onion, diced

2 cloves garlic, minced

2 tablespoons olive oil

1 jar (8 oz) oil-packed sun-dried tomatoes, drained and roughly chopped

1 cup canned crushed tomatoes

2–3 Parmesan cheese rinds (optional)

Kosher salt and freshly ground pepper

½ cup chopped fresh basil, plus whole leaves for garnish

¼ lb burrata or fresh mozzarella cheese

**SERVES 4–6**

**1** In a large skillet over high heat, combine the pasta, onion, garlic, oil, sun-dried tomatoes, crushed tomatoes, 5 cups water, Parmesan rinds (if using), and a large pinch each of salt and pepper. Bring to a boil, then reduce the heat to medium, and cook until the water is absorbed and the pasta is tender, 9–11 minutes. Remove and discard the Parmesan rinds, if using.

**2** Fold in the basil, burrata, and a large pinch each of salt and pepper. Garnish with basil and serve warm.

Parmesan rinds are an easy
way to add heartiness to
pasta sauces and soups.
Freeze rinds in an airtight
container until ready to use.

Double the spice mixture and store the extra in an airtight container to speed prep when making the dip again.

# QUESO & BEEF DIP

While technically not a supper, this dip is hearty enough to be one. You can replace the black beans with canned pintos or refried beans, and the mozzarella cheese with Monterey jack or pepper jack. If you'd like, scatter a handful of sliced black olives along with the other toppings.

**1** Preheat the oven to 425°F.

**2** In a small bowl, stir together the chili powder, cumin, oregano, garlic powder, onion powder, paprika, and 1 teaspoon salt. Set aside.

**3** In a large cast-iron skillet over medium-high heat, warm the oil. Add the ground beef and cook, stirring occasionally, until browned and cooked through, 4–6 minutes.

**4** Spoon off the excess fat from the skillet. Sprinkle the spice mixture over the beef and stir well to combine. Remove from the heat. Spoon the beans in an even layer over the beef, and sprinkle with the mozzarella and Cheddar.

**5** Transfer to the oven and bake until the cheese is melted and beginning to brown, about 10 minutes. Top the dip with the avocados, tomatoes, onion, sour cream, lime juice, and a pinch of salt, and garnish with cilantro leaves. Serve right away with tortilla chips alongside.

1 tablespoon chili powder

1½ teaspoons ground cumin

1 teaspoon dried oregano

½ teaspoon garlic powder

½ teaspoon onion powder

½ teaspoon sweet paprika

Kosher salt

2 tablespoons canola oil

1 lb ground beef

1 can (15 oz) black beans, drained and rinsed

2 cups shredded mozzarella cheese

1 cup shredded Cheddar cheese

3 avocados, pitted, peeled, and diced

2 Roma tomatoes, diced

¼ red onion, diced

⅓ cup sour cream

Juice of ½ lime

1 tablespoon fresh cilantro leaves, for garnish

Tortilla chips, for serving

**SERVES 6–8**

# BRAISED CHICKEN WITH OLIVES & ORANGE

You can trade out the cut-up whole chicken for bone-in, skin-on chicken thighs and/or breasts here. Plan on one or two pieces for each diner, depending on the appetites of your tablemates and the size of the pieces. Serve with oven-roasted potatoes.

|||||||||||||||||||||||||||||||||||||||||||||||||||||||||||||||

1 chicken (about 3 ½ lb), cut into 10 pieces

Kosher salt and freshly ground pepper

2 ½ teaspoons sweet paprika

3 tablespoons olive oil

1 yellow onion, diced

2 cloves garlic, chopped

2 teaspoons fennel seeds

¾ cup red wine

2 cups chicken broth

1 can (15 oz) diced tomatoes with juices

¾ cup black olives, such as Kalamata, pitted

Zest and juice of 1 orange (zest removed in strips with a vegetable peeler)

1 cup roasted yellow bell pepper slices

**SERVES 4**

**1** Preheat the oven to 350°F.

**2** Pat the chicken dry and season with salt and pepper. Sprinkle the chicken all over with the paprika.

**3** In a large ovenproof skillet over medium-high heat, warm 2 tablespoons of the oil. Working in batches, add the chicken and cook until browned on both sides, 8–10 minutes per batch. Transfer to a plate. Pour off the fat from the skillet.

**4** In the same skillet over medium-high heat, warm the remaining 1 tablespoon oil. Add the onion and cook, stirring occasionally, until translucent, 4–6 minutes. Add the garlic and cook, stirring occasionally, for 1 minute. Add the fennel seeds and cook, stirring occasionally, for 30 seconds. Add the wine and cook, stirring to scrape up the browned bits, until slightly reduced, about 2 minutes. Add the broth, tomatoes with their juices, olives, orange zest and juice, and bell peppers. Return the chicken to the skillet, skin side up. Make sure the top of the skin isn't covered with liquid during roasting.

**5** Transfer to the oven and roast until the chicken is tender and cooked through, 35–40 minutes. Using a slotted spoon, transfer the chicken to a plate. Place the skillet over medium-high heat and simmer until the sauce is slightly thickened, about 5 minutes. Season with salt and pepper. Return the chicken to the skillet and serve right away.

# FRITTATA WITH CHARD, SAUSAGE & FETA

Frittatas are wonderfully versatile, so view this recipe as a template. No chard in the refrigerator? Try spinach or kale in its place. Out of feta? Ricotta salata is a great substitute. Have shallots but no red onion? Use shallots instead.

**1** Place a rack in the upper third of the oven and preheat to 375°F.

**2** In a medium ovenproof nonstick skillet over medium-high heat, warm 1 tablespoon of the oil. Add the sausage and cook, stirring occasionally, until browned and cooked through, 5–6 minutes. Transfer to a paper towel–lined plate. Pour off the excess fat from the skillet.

**3** In the same skillet over medium-high heat, warm 1 tablespoon of the oil. Add the chard and cook, stirring occasionally, until just wilted, about 3 minutes. Season with salt and pepper and transfer to a plate.

**4** In the same skillet over medium-high heat, warm 1 tablespoon of the oil. Add the onion and a pinch of salt and cook, stirring occasionally, until tender and slightly translucent, about 3 minutes. Add the vinegar and cook until slightly reduced, about 2 minutes. Transfer to the plate with the chard. Wipe out the skillet to use for the frittata.

**5** In a large bowl, whisk together the eggs, milk, and a pinch each of salt and pepper. Stir in the sausage, chard, onion, and half the cheese. In the same skillet used for the onion, over medium heat, warm the remaining 1 tablespoon oil. Add the egg mixture and cook until the edges of the frittata are just set, about 2 minutes.

**6** Transfer to the oven and cook until the frittata is golden brown and set in the center, 10–15 minutes. Let cool slightly, then sprinkle with the remaining cheese, cut into wedges and serve warm.

||||||||||||||||||||||||||||||||||||||||||||||||||||||||||||||

4 tablespoons olive oil

½ lb Italian sausage, casing removed, sausage crumbled

½ bunch Swiss chard, ribs removed, leaves thinly sliced

Kosher salt and freshly ground pepper

½ red onion, cut into ½-inch dice

1 tablespoon red wine vinegar

8 large eggs

½ cup whole milk

2 oz feta cheese, crumbled

**SERVES 6–8**

# PAELLA WITH CLAMS, CHORIZO & SHRIMP

A cast-iron skillet is a kitchen workhorse, perfect for roasting, stir-frying, deep-frying, panfrying, and more. Here, it seamlessly moves into the role of paella pan, smoothly handling the cooking of each ingredient—sausages and vegetables, rice, and seafood—as it is added.

2 tablespoons olive oil

1 lb Spanish-style semicured chorizo sausages, cut into ½-inch slices

1 yellow onion, chopped

1 red bell pepper, seeded and chopped

3 cloves garlic, minced

Kosher salt and freshly ground pepper

2 cups medium-grain white rice, such as Bomba or Arborio

½ teaspoon saffron threads

4 cups chicken broth

1½ lb small clams, such as littleneck or Manila, scrubbed

1 lb large shrimp, peeled and deveined

1 cup frozen petite peas, thawed

**SERVES 4–6**

**1** In a large cast-iron skillet over medium-high heat, warm the oil. (You'll need a skillet with a lid for this recipe.) Add the chorizo and cook, turning occasionally, until browned on both sides, about 3 minutes. Add the onion, bell pepper, and garlic and cook, stirring occasionally, until softened, 3–4 minutes. Season with salt and pepper.

**2** Add the rice, crumble in the saffron, and cook, stirring, until the grains are well coated, about 2 minutes. Stir in the broth and 1½ teaspoons salt. Bring to a boil, then reduce the heat to low, cover, and cook until the rice has absorbed nearly all of the liquid, about 20 minutes.

**3** Press the clams, hinged side down, into the rice, discarding any that do not close to the touch. Spread the shrimp over the rice and scatter the peas on top. Cover and cook until the shrimp are opaque and the clams have opened, about 5 minutes. Discard any unopened clams and serve right away.

# SHORT RIB RAGOUT

If you opt for pasta with this rich, meaty sauce, choose tubes—penne, rigatoni, or paccheri—or medium-size shells to trap the sauce in the hollows. If you prefer a ribbon pasta, select a wider noodle, such as pappardelle or fettuccine.

**1** Preheat the oven to 400°F.

**2** In a large, deep ovenproof skillet over medium-high heat, warm 1 tablespoon of the oil. Working in batches, add the short ribs and cook until browned on all sides, about 2 minutes per side. Transfer to a plate. Pour off the excess fat from the skillet.

**3** In the same skillet over medium heat, warm the remaining 1 tablespoon oil. Add the onion, carrots, and celery and cook, stirring occasionally, until the vegetables are tender, 5–6 minutes. Add the garlic and cook, stirring occasionally, for 1 minute. Raise the heat to medium-high and add the wine, paprika, and cumin. Cook, stirring to scrape up the browned bits, until slightly reduced, about 5 minutes. Stir in the flour, tomato paste, mustard, and broth and bring to a simmer.

**4** Return the short ribs to the skillet, cover, and transfer to the oven. Cook until the meat is very tender, 2–2½ hours. Using tongs, transfer the short ribs to a large bowl. Place the skillet over medium-high heat and simmer until the sauce is thickened, about 15 minutes.

**5** Meanwhile, using 2 forks, shred the short ribs into bite-size pieces. Return the meat to the skillet and season with salt and pepper. Serve the ragout over pasta or mashed potatoes, and garnish with cheese and chives.

||||||||||||||||||||||||||||||||||||||||||||||||||||||||||||||||||

2 tablespoons olive oil

3 lb boneless beef short ribs

1 red onion, finely chopped

2 carrots, peeled and finely chopped

3 ribs celery, finely chopped

2 cloves garlic, minced

2 cups red wine

½ teaspoon sweet paprika

½ teaspoon ground cumin

1 tablespoon all-purpose flour

2 tablespoons tomato paste

1 tablespoon Dijon mustard

3 cups chicken or beef broth

Kosher salt and freshly ground pepper

Cooked pasta or mashed potatoes, for serving

Grated pecorino romano cheese, for garnish

Chopped fresh chives, for garnish

**SERVES 4-6**

# KOREAN CHICKEN FAJITAS

Here, a popular Tex-Mex specialty raids the Asian pantry with delicious results. For a simple side salad, toss thinly sliced cucumber with chopped green onions, rice vinegar, Asian sesame oil, and a pinch of red pepper flakes. And don't forget the ice-cold beer.

**FOR THE MARINADE**

½ cup soy sauce

½ cup mirin

2 tablespoons plus
2 teaspoons toasted
sesame oil

1 tablespoon minced garlic

1 tablespoon peeled and
minced fresh ginger

2 teaspoons firmly packed
light brown sugar

1½ lb skinless, boneless
chicken breasts, cut
into thin strips

**FOR THE SLAW**

1 cup shredded napa cabbage

⅓ cup (about 2 carrots)
peeled and shredded carrots

2 tablespoons rice vinegar

1 teaspoon honey

Kosher salt

¼ cup mayonnaise

1 tablespoon gochujang

2 tablespoons canola oil

1 red onion, thinly sliced

1 red bell pepper, seeded
and thinly sliced

6–8 flour tortillas

Cilantro sprigs, for
garnish (optional)

**SERVES 4–6**

**1** In a bowl, stir together the soy sauce, mirin, 2 tablespoons sesame oil, the garlic, ginger, and brown sugar. Add the chicken and refrigerate for 1 hour.

**2** Meanwhile, in a bowl, combine the cabbage and carrots. In a small bowl, whisk together the vinegar, the remaining 2 teaspoons sesame oil, honey, and a pinch of salt. Pour the dressing over the cabbage mixture and toss to combine. Set aside.

**3** In a small bowl, stir together the mayonnaise and gochujang and set aside.

**4** In a large cast-iron skillet over medium-high heat, warm the canola oil. Working in batches if necessary, add the chicken, onion, and bell pepper and cook, stirring occasionally, until the chicken is browned and the vegetables are soft, 2–3 minutes.

**5** Garnish with cilantro sprigs, if using, and serve the chicken and vegetables warm with the tortillas, slaw, and gochujang mayonnaise. Let diners assemble their own fajitas.

Gochujang (Korean fermented chile paste) can be found at most grocery stores in the international food aisle. If it's unavailable, use Sriracha chile sauce instead.

# INDEX

# THE SKILLET SUPPER COOKBOOK

Conceived and produced by Weldon Owen, Inc.
In collaboration with Williams-Sonoma, Inc.
3250 Van Ness Avenue, San Francisco, CA 94109

## A WELDON OWEN PRODUCTION

1045 Sansome Street, Suite 100
San Francisco, CA 94111
www.weldonowen.com

## WELDON OWEN, INC.

President & Publisher  Roger Shaw
SVP, Sales & Marketing  Amy Kaneko
Finance & Operations Director  Philip Paulick

Associate Publisher  Amy Marr

Creative Director  Kelly Booth
Associate Art Director  Lisa Berman
Senior Production Designer
   Rachel Lopez Metzger

Printed in the U.S.A.

First printed in 2016
10 9 8 7 6 5 4 3 2 1

Library of Congress Cataloging-in-Publication
data is available.

ISBN 13: 978-1-68188-136-2
ISBN 10: 1-68188-136-5

Production Director  Chris Hemesath
Associate Production Director
   Michelle Duggan
Imaging Manager  Don Hill

Photographer  Aubrie Pick
Food Stylist  Abby Stolfo
Prop Stylist  Ethel Brennen

Weldon Owen is a division of Bonnier Publishing USA

## ACKNOWLEDGMENTS

Weldon Owen wishes to thank the following people for their
generous support in producing this book: Lesley Bruynesteyn,
Penny Flood, and Bessma Khalaf